God's Perspective For Me

By Kendra Dublin

www.writersblockpublishing.net

TABLE OF CONTENTS

God is ready for us to do His will. When will you stop and yield to His purpose for your life? Every moment we are on this earth, we have the opportunity to serve God and others. Will you change your life today? Give it to God and he will direct your steps. You don't need to know where you are going because God is already there.
Where he leads you is your destiny.
Live and be free in God's will.

When I turned to God and yielded to Him, words from Him flowed to my ears, and this is what He said!

Thank you.

Purity

What do I see?
Majestic seas,
Clear and pure,
What God intended it to be
Before mankind denied serenity.
Will we go back
Or keep filling up the earth until a wasteland is all there is?
Quietness, peace, love,
Peace to the stars above.
Can I be like you and let my light shine
Maybe to a few,
Everybody that I come in contact with?
Yeah, that is the plan -
To be seen in darkness.
Come to my light,
Then you'll see God's light.
I'm going back to purity
Like the blue seas,
Clear pure and full of serenity.
I'm brushing off the dirt of sin
Because the dirt I come from is made from Him.
Back to Adam and Eve's purity;
Pollution won't ever be in me.
I'm putting out clean air
Because God is in me
And all that can come out is His majesty.

Blue Skies

Blue skies don't lie,
In God's beauty it lies.
Darkness tries to push it away,
But what God creates can't be tamed.
The creation in all its wonder
Will always tell of its King and Lord.
What else, who else can create all this?
The scientists say it came out of the sky from nothing;
We've evolved from monkeys.
It sounds so crazy
Because I was made in His image
And in His image I will return.
Not evolving from what God gave us to conquer,
But an angel that He placed on this earth.
And while I'm on this earth,
I will give what God gives to me:
Creativity in words.
God gives me His words
For me and you,
To show His perspective in me
So someone comes and bows at His glory.
I didn't do it for me;
I did it for you.
Let's go rule this world
In God's way:
In mercy and grace.

Role Model

How heavy a burden
To be everyone's light,
Waiting for my smile
To shine up your life.
How heavy a burden
To be everyone's light,
Faking it,
But making it,
To shine up your life.
How heavy a burden
To always be Jesus,
Even when I want to agree with the devil -
But who else will be Jesus?
How heavy a burden
To be your role model.
Don't look at me too closely;
Disappointment is never easy to boast.
How heavy a burden
To be your role model,
But that's what God called me to be.
So with me
We can follow
Together,
Hand in hand,
Lifting each other up
So both of us can ascend
Until His time comes.

Do you ever feel like, "All eyes are on you?"
How do you deal with the pressure?
How have you impacted the lives of others?
Have you realized you'll never be perfect, and it's okay?
If you've never felt like a role model, why not?

Rock or Sand

Rock or sand,
Stand or land
In the darkness
Of the schemer's hand.
No, stand!
Come take my hand
And shimmy out of the harsh sand.
"But what will I stand on?"
Come grab my hand.
Place your foot where I stand
Because The Rock is under me
And The Rock is above me
And in front of me,
Making sure when I lean,
Another rock forms,
Making a way out of the storm.
Now doesn't it feel better
To be standing on The Rock?
No need to brush off the dirty sand
Because now you have God's hand
And mine,
Lifting you high enough to see The Rock,
So the next steps you take
Will be on His clock.

Enough for God

Will I ever be enough for you, Lord?
Am I enough for you now
Or are you waiting for my breakthrough?
Am I sitting on my breakthrough?
No, I haven't arrived,
But I'm living for you.
What more can I do?
Required to do this,
But isn't my life supposed to be bliss?
Well, I don't know.
But there must be more in me.
Isn't that why I'm still living?
What purpose would I have on this earth
If I've reached my destiny?
So the questions stands:
Am I enough?
Am I doing enough?
Yes, to the first.
No, to the second.
Yeah, I can do more -
Especially with God in me,
Planting his seeds
So more comes out of me.
No, dying of me.

Do you often feel like you aren't enough?
Will you ever realize that we can never be or do enough?
What is the definition of grace?
Are you walking in God's purpose?
If so, what does that look like? If no, why not? Are you ready to change now?
If you said yes and couldn't explain your answer, are you really living in your purpose?

Like You

Lord, help me to be more like you -
Not so critical,
But free-spirited in love.
Why so down?
Why so annoyed?
You prepared me for these times,
No need to feel a void.
Consumed with anger,
A little despair,
Get over it -
And just flick your hair.
I will be more like you.
Maturity is clue
The more I study the book of true -
I'm becoming more like you.

What do you do the second you feel annoyed or angry?
Do you indulge in those feelings or talk to God?
Do you bring others into your situation?
How much quicker would you get over things or find resolutions if you
talked to God first?
Are some things so small that you can let them go in the moment?

Deliverance or Delivery

Deliverance!
No, delivery.
Can I have my blessing in 30 minutes,
A few hours?
Can't wait for God to devour,
Thinking of a plan to change the ending.
Why haven't I heard the doorbell ring?
Despair, well I guess you don't care.
Maybe my home girl will have a resolution -
Nah, all that'll come out of her is pollution.
Well, maybe I'll just handle this trial myself
Because every time I pray, I'm not getting help.
I feel a little comfort as I vent to the Lord,
But I want my delivery -
Okay, my deliverance - by the 4th
Because the 1st already came
But I can't be late for the 5th.
By the end of that day
There's going be a blizzard,
Hail, thunder.
Lord, just take me six feet under.
But what will be left of me -
A girl who lost while exiting?
Go ahead, Lord, take the wheel.
Let me buckle up.
Are we there yet?
God, why are you going straight?
You missed your turn.
"Be quiet.
Today you're gon' learn.
I know what you need;
My purpose will never flee.
Now do as I say,
And let me be God Almighty."

Honestly, what do you prefer - a quick delivery or deliverance? Is there
a difference?
How does your life reflect your answer?
How patient are you in a trial?
Do you give God ultimatums?
How do you talk to God, family, and friends during a trial?

My Mind or God's

My mind or God of my mind?
No, I'll stand blind,
Only to walk into a pit.
It wasn't too hard to find.
Darkness is funny
Because right after daylight,
Here it comes -
Just like a snake,
Moving slowly until it takes its prey.
Just when I thought I'd won the victory,
Self-righteousness came to blind me.
On the road to Damascus
Is where God wanted to turn me around,
But I kept moving into sinking ground,
Thinking of how God blessed me,
Only to say, "No, that was all me."
Like I made the day
Or the winds to blow,
Like I created myself,
The trees, ocean boundaries.
Yeah, give it up -
You'll never have God's majesty
Or even come close.
What a lesson to boast!
And that's when I saw little light.
And when I saw that rope come down,
I thought I could do a little climbing.
It seemed much quicker falling down.
Step by step,
Right hand over left,
Getting out of that pit was all I needed to quit
And humble myself to God,
For He is what makes all great things happen.
Now for this rocky road,
I am fit!

Do you often find yourself praising yourself versus praising God?
Why do you act like you're God?
How long will it take for you to humble yourself?

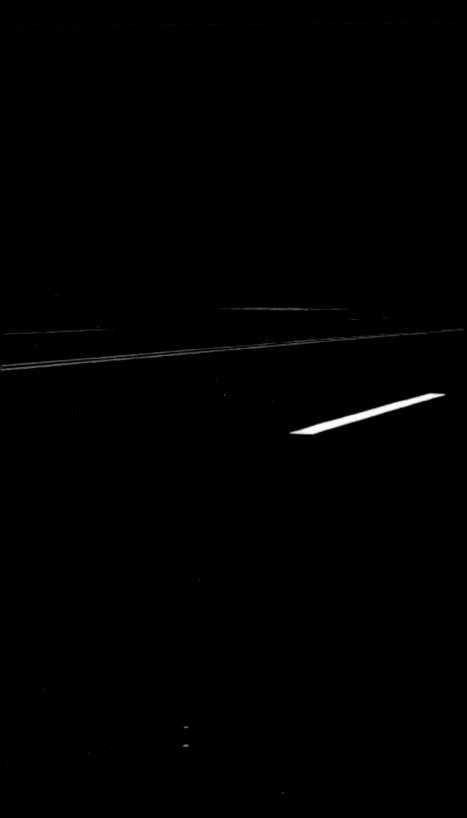

Drive Drunk

Drive sober!
No, I'm looking for someone to kill.
Not my thoughts,
But my actions speaking.
Drive sober!
No, drive drunk.
I drive better with a few in me.
Where do you want to go?
I can take you to Heaven or Hell,
At the end of this journey that's where we will be.
How else will I stop unless I die?
Die together,
Two funerals -
More like 10.
So many more souls on this road other than you and me.
Lord, take me home safely.
I want to live!
I can't see anymore.
My mind is dead;
Drive me home, Lord.
Allow your angels to drive me home.

Salt Water

Salt of the earth,
Water for replenishing.
I feel more like dirt,
Waiting for another trampling.
I lost my saltiness a long time ago,
Hanging with wrong people.
Flavor exited my soul.
Dull, torn down,
Flawless, not now -
Ages ago.
That person has gone
Like I never knew her at all.
Water to replenish,
More like alcohol running through my veins
With every pulse.
Where my body goes,
I don't know
Because I am a desert,
My body holding heat.
But no water to set me free
So I can be me -
But maybe this is me.
No, God didn't plan this for me.
This alcohol has me living,
But I'm all dried up -
Bland, tasteless.
A little Aquafina might save this hangover,
But that won't be enough.
I want the Lord to come over and amplify me.
I'm tired of being a weary land.
I want God's water to run through my feet to my hands,
And sprinkle a little salt.
I know plenty remains.
Now I'm hydrated and tasty;
Now it's time to figure out what God has for me.

What were some of your lowest moments?
How did you feel?
Have you gotten out of that situation, or are you still in it?
What steps are you taking to trust in God and be one with Him?
What was the purpose for talking to God? What are you doing now as a result of it?
Are you ready to give your life to Christ?

Misery

Even in my misery,
I knew God was going to comfort me.
So lost,
But I knew God was there for me.
I left me
Like my spirit left,
And looked at my dead body.
Why do you keep doing this to yourself?
Drink after drink,
Sex, no rest,
Living nightlife's test.
Testing what I'm made of -
How far can you go?
Another drink,
But you're in control.
When will I rest?
Oh girl, look at that dress.
Yeah, I heard my ex will be there.
So let's go downtown
And let it flow,
Whatever will be.
Open the door to my sanctuary;
The dance floor is calling my name.
Everyone thinking,
"Is that the same girl from high school days?
She's changed.
No God in her."
So who's to blame...
Me.
I let my soul grow ugly,
Untamed and ashamed.
But then I remembered the only name:
Prince of Peace.
Then I heard,
"Kendra Dublin, come back to me
And let my spirit flow in thee."
Yes, Lord, I'm ready.
Show me the steps to take.
I'm ready to come home;
No more spring break.

Lose Me

Keep losing me so I can become me,
But I don't want to become who God created me to be.
I like holding on to bitterness, Hate.
I kind of like the savagery in me.
Every time someone comes for me,
I'll scream and holler like a lion
Because God's humanity isn't in me. So why try?
Maybe Darwin got it right.
Yeah, I like this me.
Living a life of purpose, for what?
I want to have fun however I see fit:
Drinking, partying, sexing,
I mean; who would want to give up all that?
My Instagram would fall flat
If I started posting about God.
Who really wants to see that?
And whoever is posting about Him is lying;
Nobody these days is good.
So what's the use in trying? No, I think I like this me.
I don't want to learn another lesson.
No more time for stressing
Because I'm going to do I want to do.
Because when I went to church, I opened up the doors.
I saw plenty of people needing healing.
No, hypocrisy is what I saw -
Saying one thing and doing another. So why would I go any further?
It's not in me to fake and front,
But then again, is this really the life I want?
I don't know.
Maybe I just need someone to talk to.
Maybe I just need a new crew.
My best friend asked me if I wanted to go to her church,
But I brushed it off and started talking about my mess,
That I didn't have time to be blessed.
Blessed, yeah.
Why can't I be blessed?
She's always saying how God is blessing her and I see it,
But will He really do the same for me?
Well, I guess it wouldn't hurt to try it again,
Maybe all of her girls can be my friends.
Yeah, I'll go. Here goes nothing. No, here goes something.

Have you moved on from the "old you?"
Do you feel like it's a constant struggle?
Are you more judgmental than you would like to be?
What are the world's view on judgement and how does it differ from
God's view? Which side are you on?
What will you do to become more like Christ?

I Need Healing

God is healing me.
Broken, torn apart,
But He's sewing me up;
He's healing and massaging my heart.
Why won't this day pass?
I thought trouble didn't last.
This pain is too much to bear -
Maybe I'll call him up.
He can hold me and caress my hair.
Yes, that's what I'll do…
But no, I deleted his number.
I knew my insanity would start to speak in a few.
One small victory for me,
But why does my heart bleed?
Is it because I took it out if my chest
Only to realize his blood wouldn't sustain mine?
My blood type is O; His is undefined.
Or maybe it is defined, it's just not pumping into mine.
Why did I pour so much of me
Until I was empty
And he was filled with me?
I didn't allow God to fill me with living water,
So as I was poured into, more was coming in, overflowing.
This is why I'm empty.
By George, I think I've got it!
God is who I need to give my heart to -
Not someone who has no clue
Of the greatness that I am.
Who provides all we need
Like the Israelites?
Giving manna in the desert to keep them healthy,
Free of need.
I give my heart to you, God - And only you.
Keep healing me, upgrade me.
And the man you provide will match my love for thee.
Let's pour into each other, no droughts.
But when it is time to work things out,
God is our third spouse.

What was the hardest break up you've dealt with?
How did it impact you initially?
Where you lost, broken, or confused?
Did you allow you boyfriend to be your God?
What signs did God give you to leave before things got worse?
What steps did you take to heal and become whole again or for the first time?
What will you do differently in your next relationship or before it?
Will you give yourself time for you?

The Beginning

The past doesn't last,
But it's here today.
But didn't that day pass away?
But it's in my mind to stay.
Replaying the great times,
Only to be met with its disastrous ending.
A relationship that ended with a baby pending.
To be a murderer?
Or not a murderer?
To murder means the growing pains of a child is brushed away.
I'm free of that responsibility;
No more yesterday -
Only to be awakened at night
With a baby's cry.
But didn't that baby pass away?
Will I forever be in pain and misery?
Probably.
Covering up one sin with another,
Depression overtaking me.
Why not kill me?
I killed my baby.
God will hear my baby's cry over me.
What could it be?
A boy or girl?
A possible Olympian like my girl Ashley?
A writer like me and my daddy?
For this cruel sin,
Will I be in recovery?
No.
No more need to flash to the future
Because I'm keeping my baby.
I can't do this.
A relationship gone wrong will be the only thing I carry
Until God frees me from this pain.
Every day will get better.
Plus, I have a little me in me.
What a beautiful journey this will be!

Have you ever been faced with the decision to terminate a pregnancy?
What did you say to yourself to justify the termination or to keep your
baby?
What did your family and friends say to you? What did God say? What
did you say to Him?
Have you healed from it?
Will you get past it?
Have you given your load to God?

Alternate Ending

The past doesn't last,
But it's here today.
But didn't that day pass away?
But it's in my mind to stay.
Replaying the great times,
Only to be met with its disastrous ending.
A relationship that ended with a baby pending.
To be a murderer?
Or not a murderer?
To murder means the growing pains of a child is brushed away.
I'm free of that responsibility;
No more yesterday.
Only to be awakened at night
With a baby's cry.
But didn't that baby pass away?
Will I forever be in pain and misery?
Probably. covering up one sin with another,
Depression overtaking me.
Why not kill me?
I killed my baby.
God will hear my baby's cry over me.
What could it be?
A boy or girl?
A possible Olympian like my girl Ashley?
A writer like me and my daddy?
For this cruel sin
Will I be in recovery?
Well, it is what it is.
My appointment is at 3:30 p.m.
As I sit before the procedure,
I can't believe what I'm about to do.
But I'll get through because I can't pay for two.
Three months later,
Lord, what did I do?
I can't get out of this coma.
Why did I oppose you?
I can't sleep,
I can't eat,
The grief is too much to bear.
Lord, I know you're there.
I repent; I've sinned against you.
Comfort me,
Hold me tonight,
Surround me.
My mind, my body.
Then Jesus spoke to me,
"I'm here.
Grace and mercy will never flee.
I'll save you from your shaming.

Shake You

God shakes you
To wake you up.
Up, up, and away you go.
He wants you to reach your goals,
But no -
You'd rather sleep in despair.
Wake up and see that God is there!
Every day we're getting closer to His return.
Why would you want to burn?
Why not yearn for a life of hope?
Going through a trial
So you can see the vital
Parts of life.
Stressing never helps the fight.
Give it to Him.
You're a conquer;
You'll win.

Do you need God to shake you up right now?
Are you living a purpose filled life or are you just existing?
What will it take for you to realize that God will make you successful
when you are elevating Him?
What are your talents or spiritual gifts?
What are you willing to do beginning today to walk in your ministry? List
some practical steps to guide you.

3rd Semester

Third trimester,
The end of a long semester.
Will all my hard work pay off?
Is there a book that I could've written?
A word of encouragement that could have been spoken to myself?
Why have I lived this long and lived half my purpose?
I know what else God has placed in me,
But if everything isn't my way,
Words on the page will not be unveiled.
All my books will be word of mouth.
I could've made my mark,
But maybe I'm all burned out.
Does God really want me to leave this earth
Without doing everything He placed in me? No.
But that'll probably be,
So as I give birth to my soul passing on,
I'll remember this song:
"Almost doesn't count."

Weave in Me

Weave yourself in me, Lord.
Intertwine yourself in me, Lord.
Move in me,
In and out of my body until
There is no me, Lord.
Put your love in me
Like a straitjacket so I can't leave.
Stitch me up in your mercy;
Surge me up in your grace.
Bind me up in your love;
I don't want to be free from you.
Don't let me go,
Like your promise made in a rainbow.

What does it mean for God to weave in you?
Have you allowed God to weave in you?
Will you trust God with all that you have?

Naked and Unafraid

Naked and unafraid,
Free and unashamed,
Floating and quoting.
All that God is saying,
Hoping and praying,
Listening and waiting.
Pure and ready to leave the pain of sin
That won't take me down again.
I'm all the way up!
The ground is too low for my flow;
I'm flying high in divine time.
Wherever you lead, Lord, I'll go.

Happy to be Me

Happy to be me,
Living free.
Yeah, its Kendra Dublin coming -
Who else would it be?
Moving and shaking,
Loving is key.
Loving who I am
Just because I'm me:
Silly, crazy, dramatic,
A free spirit -
Yeah, that's me.
Moving through life organically,
Never living through another being.
Who do you think you are?
I told you, it's me!
Whatever nickname you choose
Just depends on what time of life you met me,
But everybody has seen
The same ole me.
Loving life
Because I know who I was made to be,
So I'm living in my destiny.

Are you happy to be you? Why or why not?
What has hindered you from accepting who you are and what God has given you to offer to the world?
When others try to hold you down? How do you respond? Do you believe them or ignore them?
Do you believe your gift is good enough?

I Believe in Me

You don't have to believe in me;
I believe in me!
God gave me this purpose,
So you're free to leave in peace.
You don't have to believe in me;
I know I'm the next big thing.
Stop putting your doubts and fears into my hearing.
You don't have to believe in me,
But you should believe in God.
He's the catalyst,
The gift I just unwrapped.
Will give words to save the lost,
Encouragement to the forgotten,
Healing to the unforgettable sin.
So I'm gonna do me.
Well, I'm gonna do the God in me.
You can't bind this free being,
So no more devaluing of what God's placed on my path.
Find peace in your grace, your gift,
And in the aftermath, the next time you see me,
We can embrace because we are living in Christ.
Whatever He placed in you can help my walk my life.

Competition

Competition -
With whom?
There's room for you and you,
Not just a few.
God is in all,
My friend.
I want you to win,
So I won't hinder you.
If you need help,
My hand is in.
If prayer is all you require,
I'll lift your name higher.
Now use the power God gave you
And as I uplift you.
God will bless two!

Do you feel like you are in competition with friends, family, or church members?
Is it fun or detrimental to be in competition with others?
How do you handle competition?
How will you overcome competition?

My Friend

Friends to the end,
Until Christ came in.
I want to change;
You continue to drown in sin.
But I'm here!
Don't you see my hand in the water?
Can you see?
Are you reaching out to be saved?
I want to help you get out.
I'm here!
Don't say, "Go away."
Just the pains of our friendship change.
We can be friends to the end,
But it won't be the same
Since you say Christ doesn't reign.
Why not bow with me?
I'll help you see.
Friends to the end,
I want to see you believe,
Become free, and leave a life of destruction.
I hope you see someday.
Until then, we'll be friends to the end,
But here's where the boundaries begin
And will remain,
Because I've evolved.
I have to listen to God's call.

Have any of your friendships been strained after you come to Christ?
What are some of the differences?
Have you cut some of your friends off?
If so, where else will they see God?
Can you have still have a relationship with them even though you have
different beliefs?

Take Me Away

Take me away
To Heaven's gate.
Take me away
To God,
To the Lamb that was slain.
Seems so far away,
I guess I'll have a little bit of heaven
While I'm on this earth.
Shining your light
Since my rebirth.
Take me away
To Heaven's wonder.
Streets of gold,
No need for thunder.
Just God's voice,
No need to be afraid.
My spirit in your spirit,
Now everything is golden.
But until then,
I'll sing your name,
Your name I will proclaim,
So on that beautiful day,
When your spirit is in sight,
I'll see how wondrous is your light.
Now I'm home.
I'm finally home.

Sunny on the Inside

Wake up!
Pray to God for waking me up;
Get ready to start the day.
Then I hear a little rain.
I look out and most would say,
"Lord, take this rain away."
But I don't mind because I'm
Sunny on the inside.
I get to work
And the store is in disarray,
My opener is late,
And at the last minute, there's a promotional change.
But it's all good, because I'm
Sunny on the inside.
While on my break,
I check my phone.
My boyfriend says, "I need some space."
Then I think, what can I do to make him stay?
But then again, he's not right for me anyways.
My future is looking brighter already because I'm
Sunny on the inside.
I leave from work
And the sun is shining so bright.
I'm on my way home;
I have conquered another work day.
I'm on the highway and the driver behind me thought,
"Let me ruin her day."
An accident that didn't have to be.
Why couldn't you have texted your friend later in the evening?
Then I thank the Lord
I'm still living, so I'm definitely
Sunny on the inside.
When I make it home I think,
Where will I get the money for the deductible?
Then I remember, you are debt free.
Don't you remember setting aside money back in February?
Thank you, God, for disciplining me.
With raining eyes, I'm feeling
Sunny on the inside.
When God shines in your life,
You won't go around in sorrow.
Every day is a gift,
No word from tomorrow.
So live for today!
Smile and tell someone,
"It's going be okay."
Until I meet Him on that day,
His light will be within my body -
So I'm sunny on the inside!

You Are Not God

Take me from the presence of God?
You must be kidding!
I don't want a distraction;
I need a blessing.
Any man who wants to sit at my dad's table
Better be alive in the spirit and able
To help me in my walk.
God is alive in me and is ready to talk.
I can't stop my purpose for you!
So, if I need to,
I will show you away
Into a dead lady,
Because I'm not on my way to the grave.
Honey, I'm living!
So before we get started, I'm just going let you go
Because the spirit is elevating me.
I can take you there,
But you aren't ready to let go.
"I see the world;
I don't see God."
That's not true
Because you see me.
What other proof do you need?
But I'll let you be free
In death.
Tonight, you won't rest,
Since you'll be thinking of me -
The woman who can help you be.
But you aren't ready.
It's all good because I'm not waiting,
But I am waiting on the one that God's going to send in my pathway.
And fast forwarding to when we are old and grey,
We'll be able to say,
"We LIVED together.
Our lives were not in vain.
Look at all the seeds we watered.
I'm at peace with seeing the Heavenly Father."

Have you ever dated someone who tried to take you away from God?
If so, did you consider it or were you prepared to stand firm in your
faith?
Would you stick around to persuade them in the faith?

The Trees and Me

The trees of the Lord are well-watered,
Like me.
Seeking nourishment from the rain,
Being filled with all they need
To sustain,
To grow.
Ready for any harsh weather
Because the foundation is firm.
Keep filling me up, God, like the trees.
Replenishing me every day
As I read your word and pray.
Our relationship is reaching new heights.
I'm getting a sneak peak of Heaven daily.
Even when it rains
And situations flood my life,
You pull back the waters that came up to my neck
That try to drown me.
But I don't fret,
As I see the ocean start to recede.
I was only being tested;
You allow me to grow through humility.
If God can separate the sky and seas,
He can definitely separate me from Satan's thinking.
Shower me with your love;
You know what I need.
As I live in my purpose, I'm starting to see,
Because once the waters started to recede,
There is so much open space, like I am free
And ready to get back to we -
God and me.
But why did I wait so long?
I could've gotten out of that storm when I was knee-deep.
I guess it's because I could still see most of my body
And didn't think the flood would move so quickly.
All that I was supposed to see was God,
So every other day that's all I see.
As I write to tell His story,
I'm becoming more like the Great I Am -
The Alpha and Omega,
The Bright and Morning Star,
The Light and The Rock,
So in my purpose, I will never stop.

Brewing in Me

The spirit is brewing in me,
Like a pot of water screaming,
"Get me out of here!
I'm too hot to stay.
I've reach my temperature;
Release me now."
My purpose has started.
God is brewing in me like a volcano
As the earth beneath heats up
And the rocks turn into magma,
Waiting for an opening.
Seeping into one chamber;
Rising to the surface and erupt to say,
"Here I am!
It's been a long time coming."
I'm growing in God
Like a gift from a mother's belly.
Morning sickness,
Something feels different in me
Month after month.
Receiving food and nourishment
To help the baby grow.
Turning and tossing.
Developing hands, toes, mouth, organs
Needed for life -
And nine months later, ready to see the world.
I have to get out of here.
It's my turn!
God is living in me
Like Jesus started His journey preparing for His mission,
Being filled with the scriptures,
Ready to show God's glory,
Telling all the way to the Kingdom
God sent Jesus.
We needed His grace.
It was time for the Healer, the Lamb.
Now God is unleashing me!
My boiling point has come;
I'm finally ready for His itinerary.
Who is being healed today by your words through me?
Give them what I tell you, and they will come to me.
Now I'll prepare them for their boiling point.

Have you ever felt like you were actually walking in God's purpose?
Do you know for what purpose you were placed on this earth?
Have you ever felt like you could do anything in God?
Will you get on God's path and live the life He has panned for you?
Will you go as Abraham did when God calls you? Will you keep no plans
other than those of God?

Life Long Marathon

I've trained all my life,
Now it's time to run a marathon.
I've ran the 100, 200,
One mile, even two -
But the marathon is where God blesses through and through.
I see you clearer and clearer,
No time for a break.
God's water will sustain!
I see the hallway point;
I can't be late.
Another blessing is ahead of me today.
I've studied; I've walked in His light.
But the 200 wasn't enough.
I realized I couldn't sprint through life
And I stopped the fight.
After winning the gold, I was thinking everything was fine,
Long enough to believe that walking was divine.
Not for me.
You can do this in your sleep;
You've seen it in your dreams.
Don't lose your life -
So run, baby, run!
I'm catching up to the Son,
The One who guides and keeps His promises
The same way He promised Abraham, Isaac and Jacob.
Obediently finishing the race,
On time and in line with God's will
Until His heavenly light is revealed.
Oh, how my spirit is filled!

ABCs of God

Are you really living the life God wants:
Bringing souls to Christ?
Communing with His people?
Devoting your time to learning Him?
Elevating your mind to a new high?
Freely giving of your gift?
Going where God tells you to go?
Helping others to see God?
Imagine if all of us lived for God,
Joining our talents into a powerful ministry.
Keeping all of his command,
Letting go and forgiving,
Mending and healing,
Never settling.
Overcoming with every step.
Putting the devil in his place;
Quickly seeing and blocking the enemy.
Revealing all that God is telling you;
Showing the children what it means to be a witness.
Telling all of His goodness;
Understanding and giving the grace of God.
Vowing to never leave;
Warming your heart to every person's plea.
Xystering the layers of sin;
Yearning for the day that all will be saved.
Zesting the world with salt and the light of day!

Thank You

Thank you, God,
For all the many words I never knew I had,
Giving me peace,
Knowing you will always provide.
Don't be nervous -
Out of my mouth,
Your words will fly
Into the ears of man,
Into the ears of the devil.
Saying, "No, you can't have me,
Because I'm living in His purpose."
Showing me you'll come
In your Divine timing.
Showing me who rules this world.
You made this earth in six days:
The ocean, the land,
The sky, the animals.
But you can't give me a few words to rhyme?
How crazy of me
To think anything less.
Your words will never stop flowing
I hear you say, "Keep going.
Until you reach your destination.
No, until you reach my destination.
I gave you those gifts,
So your gifts will always be."
Five turning into 10,
10 turning into 20,
Give me that extra talent.
I'll know what to do!
I just have to hear your words,
Keep multiplying
Until I see you!

How often do you give yourself time to realize what God has done?
Do you turn off the television or turn off your phone?
When is the last time you cried, sang, or worshipped God other than
during church service?

Physical Body

Physical body
Won't always be.
The grief of a loved one
Is only the beginning
Because all the physical body can do is provide shelter for the soul.
And while the soul is in the body,
The spirit protects the soul,
Keeping a close watch
Day after day,
Right or wrong,
God or Satan.
Which way will I go?
The spirit is in control.
And as the body grows old,
Or your purpose had been fulfilled on earth,
The physical will have to go.
Boldly saying, "Not yet,
I want to stay!"
But realizing the clock won't change,
So as we grieve along the way.
Remember, God's not done yet.
All the body could do is provide mortal support as we bowed down on
this earth.
If we do,
Then our destiny is with you, God.
So no more crying for my body;
My spirit is abiding in Him.

Live in Peace

Rest in peace.
No, live in peace!
My body is dead,
But my spirit is living,
Waiting to be called into Heaven,
Where all the saints will be present.
Oh, yes!
I'm going to live in peace,
In the land of eternal beings,
Praising God,
No need for healing
Because we are all made new
In His spirit.
My soul is rejoicing!
The location of me
Doesn't matter because God has me.
So until judgment day,
I'm living in peace.
Oh, what a feeling to be separated from the body!
No more burdens to carry,
No more shell holding me back,
Now I'm closer to the Father.
So don't cry, because I'm still living.
I might not be watching over you,
But you have God.
What more do you need?
Just pray on that day
We'll unite in worship every day.
Live your life;
Don't stop for me
Because I'm living in peace!

Dear Satan

Why do you hate me?
Is it because you see God in me?
The way I move,
The way I talk,
You want to be me.
Misery loves company,
So you want to sift me,
See what I'm made of.
Oh, but did you forget?
God made me
And that's all you'll see.
You had the chance;
You lived in His kingdom.
You thought you could be God,
But He showed you
There's only one me.
You know you're already defeated.
Trying to take me with you
Like I should follow you.
How many souls can I take with me?
But my spirit is free.
You know you can't win,
So give up and return to the dirt.
Let me be!
But no, misery loves company.
But I don't want no new friends,
So go away and don't come back another day.
But if you do, just know -
That battle, you're going to lose.
So sift me.
All that will be left is a better me:
Stronger in God,
A new being.

Do you feel like Satan is always attacking?
How do you handle your trials?
Do you feel defeated most of the time?
How will you allow God to fight the battle so you can become stress-
free?

True Worship

We will worship together in Heaven,
But it's sad that we can't do it on earth.
We let technicalities break us,
Separate us,
And even those we can't stand on
Since those aren't concrete.
We tell each other,
"You are going to Hell,"
Because we don't do things the same.
We don't worship the same,
And say,
"God didn't say that."
So what is He saying to you?
Be me?
Certainly not!
I can just imagine
All Christians coming together
From all walks of life,
From every country.
There wouldn't be a place big enough to hold us.
But then again, we are the church.
So let's just stand outside.
It would be so amazing!
Proclaiming Jesus is the son of God,
Worshiping Him,
Giving Him the glory,
Singing and lifting our hands towards Heaven.
Oh, what a sight to see!
Nothing could shake us.
So powerful
The world would have to stop and take notice.
CNN, MSNBC,
Let's go and see.
I want to be a part of that beauty;
Let's hear what God has to say to me.
Isn't this what God wanted?
Why must we break what was made whole
And be so bold about it?
Oh, how I wish it could be,
But the reality is there are some things I won't see on this earth.
But thanks be to God, my time in Heaven is coming!

If you're inspired, write your own poems, notes, responses, short stories, drawings, math problems, jokes, or anything. Just write!

Notes:

Notes:

Notes:

Notes:

Made in the USA
Middletown, DE
22 April 2017